T0269906

Ikebana

The Zen Way of Flowers

Yuji Ueno

TUTTLE Publishing

Tokyo | Rutland, Vermont | Singapore

CONTENTS

Why I Wrote This Book

My first encounter with ikebana was at an exhibition. Strongly affected by the stirring works, I began learning ikebana. However, I was still young, and being so energetic at the time, feeling a sense of empathy or projecting onto the flowers was unthinkable.

The way I dealt with flowers altered because of significant changes in my own mind. After various experiences of being stuck in both public and private life, my feelings toward not only flowers but also plants in general changed dramatically. I began to think and muse about how to empathize with plants and how to project this onto my work. From there, I started to feel the importance of deciding and thinking about things in a simpler way.

When working with plants becomes an occupation and part of the everyday, the very act of looking at plants becomes distorted with the passage of time. With human greed and dependence on others comes the prideful desire to create something different and surprising, sometimes resulting in excessive use of flowers and an overly artificial effect, whereas arranging flowers is really very simple. Even a single flower is sufficient to make an impression and convey thoughts.

I hope that this book will inspire readers to face flowers in a simple way.

About the Term "Hanaike"

I began to use the term "hanaike" (flower arranging) experimentally about fifteen years ago as the noun for works of plant arrangements. This word did not originally mean "the act of arranging flowers." In the world of ikebana, it was used as another name for "vase." When I was first thinking about connecting on equal terms with other flower arrangers around the world, works of all kinds were being subsumed by the contemporary English term "floral arrangements," which was inconsistent with the image I was trying to convey. As a term that wasn't too far removed from the image of ikebana, I began using "hanaike." Back when I started experimenting with using "hanaike," originally a noun, as a verb, and as the noun for an arrangement, the use of "hanaike" to mean "the act of arranging flowers" began to become more and more widely known. It is my hope that "hanaike" will become a commonly understood term to connect flower arrangers across the world.

Chapter 1

LOOKING AT FLOWERS/ ARRANGEMENTS WITH A SINGLE TYPE OF FLOWER

Arranging Flowers

When I began learning ikebana, I was taught "never let a flower bloom without a name." This is because in the world of ikebana, flower names are part of the learning, and it is important to take into account the names and backgrounds of flowers. While I don't deny this, I personally think it is fine to use flowers with which one is not particularly familiar. Certainly, when arranging flowers, it's important to learn about the environment in which they grow, their form, the source of their name and so on, and draw on this understanding in order to work. However, I think that the impulse that draws us to a certain flower that happens to be blooming and makes us want to touch it and arrange it is extremely important. By arranging flowers, we can come to know them and the natural environment of their native habitat, share the stirring emotions we receive from plants, and develop a respect for nature. The most important thing is to encounter flowers that inspire in us the desire to know and learn about them.

Looking at Flowers

Before arranging, it's important to properly face the flowers you will be using. When I've bought flowers from a market or flower shop and am going to arrange them, before staring I always pick out the ones that tug at my heartstrings. When there are several stalks of rose of the same species and color, they all look the same at a glance. Particularly for those who are not accustomed to flower arranging, everything looks the same at the start. But when you look carefully, it becomes clear that even within the same species, there are subtle differences. Gaze at the face of a flower to take in its stalk, leaves, and overall form. Especially when arranging just one type of flower, understand the overall balance and look at them from front-on again. Then select the ones you find interesting or attractive or that stir your heart. Sometimes, once the arrangement is finished, you might feel it's not quite right. At those times, it's fine to alter your selection.

The important thing is to really face flowers properly and not choose them in a rush or out of habit. The more often you face flowers, the more they will speak to you.

Distance from Flowers

When choosing flowers to arrange, start by holding them and checking them at close range. Once you've started arranging them, make sure to look at them from a degree of distance. This is an important step for checking not only the flowers for arrangement, but also the vessel and place in which they will be displayed, along with the overall balance. It may happen that you choose a flower with a lot of foliage and, when holding it, think it will be attractive arranged with the leaves as they are; however, once you view the arrangement at a slight distance, the green of the foliage overwhelms the flower. With some distance, it's possible to sense if the leaves overwhelm, and make the decision to remove some of them.

By creating a little distance between yourself and the flowers, you'll be able to see more clearly what it is that you want to express and convey. This is true for flowers but also very helpful when arranging items such as branches and twigs. When arranging flowers, there's a tendency to look only at the form directly in front of one's eyes. Looking at things from a slight distance makes the shape of the twigs clearer and it becomes easier to know which twigs and foliage need tidying up. Taking a step back and looking calmly at the arrangement is also reflecting on it. The accumulation of these reflections leads to good hanaike.

Values Placed on Flowers

When arranging flowers, there's no need to stick to those sold in shops. Of course, the flowers grown by top producers are magnificent, but there are flowers all around us, not only in shops. Personally, I buy them at flower markets, but I don't stick to cut flowers—I often arrange pieces I've cut from seedlings or potted plants. Sometimes I make use of garden blooms or wildflowers growing by the side of the road. In this book, I even use the invasive species *Coreopsis lanceolata*. As long as it stirs your heart, I think it's fine to use whatever flower you like.

Once when I went to America, I was taken to a place where there were clusters of Japanese knotweed, which is known in Japan as an invasive species. In Japan, it is considered a nuisance, but the American who took me around said "Isn't this a lovely flower?" Even though in Japan they are invasive and destroy the habitat of native species, in their native habitat they are beloved as wildflowers. In other words, the value placed on flowers as beautiful or charming is significantly influenced by the viewer's environment or beliefs. Draw on your own values to select flowers.

Anthropomorphizing Flowers

Hanaike is a projection of oneself. It's astonishing how much of oneself is projected into arrangements—when I'm in high spirits, I use flowers that are full of energy, and when I'm feeling down, I choose ones with a more somber air. This is because we unwittingly perceive flowers as anthropomorphic. To me, lilies, chrysanthemums, camellias and so on are flowers that are easily likened to human figures.

The act of plucking wildflowers by hand, which has continued since time immemorial, is an act of possession, of making the flowers one's own. It is said that it began with greed, with humans then going on to wear flowers and display them in their dwellings. This may be a manifestation of the desire to project oneself onto a beautiful flower or to imitate its beauty. People have long likened flowers to themselves or their loved ones. It's fair to say that we have come to express ourselves through flowers. In other words, through arranging flowers, we gain a deeper understanding of ourselves and others, and this is connected to the expression of hanaike.

Narcissus Jonquilla

Flower: Narcissus Jonquilla
Vessel: Aoki Ryo | White Porcelain | Small pot
Season: Winter - Early Spring

Narcissus Jonquilla is a seasonal standard floral element in ikebana from December to February, when the new year is celebrated. It's often used together with its long leaves, but in this instance, the lidded vessel used is small, so I've kept the leaf length moderate. I've arranged the flowers, which are in full bloom, in front of the upward-reaching leaves. Jonquils bloom in clusters, so I've arranged one cluster over the other to connect them, with the lower flowers facing slightly down and the upper flowers facing to the front. The classical air of the jonquils combine with the delicate quality of the pot for a look that is charming but has a sophistication to it.

Camellia Japonica

Camellias are the first flowers to color the still chilly air of early spring. Native to Japan, they grace my garden and I love to see them bloom. The flowers themselves are large and easy to anthropomorphize, which is another reason I want to arrange them.

This pale pink camellia is one that blossomed in my garden, so there is some slight damage to the petals near the center, but this adds to its charm. In order to bring out its charm, I selected a unique glass vase with a gentle air.

Flower: Camellia Japonica
Vessel: Noto Asana | Glass | Vase
Season: Winter - Spring

Petunia

When arranging just one flower or one species, that flower's presence is heightened. The clearer you are about what you want to convey or express, the more clearly it will come across.

Here, I've used a black double-blossom petunia. I've used one that was raised in a pot, so it's interesting that the stem has not grown straight. In order to clearly convey that, I have chosen a tall vessel to create an arrangement that shows the growth trajectory of the plant.

Flower: Petunia Black Pearl
Vessel: Anzai Kenta | Ceramic | Vase
Season: Spring - Summer

Dianthus Superbus var. longicalycinus

Japanese women are often referred to as being like the *Dianthus superbus var. longicalycinus* (also called the fringed pink or large pink). It's been a popular flower since olden times. Arranging this stem, which is not straight, but rather inclined slightly to the right, in a vessel that has warmth to it emphasizes the pink's delicacy and unpretentious loveliness. The mouth of the vessel is wide, so the flower is held in place with a single twig across the vase opening.

Flower: Dianthus Superbus var. longicalycinus (large pink)
Vessel: Antique | China | Handmade earthenware
Season: Spring - Summer

Ipomoea Purpurea

Flower: Ipomoea Purpurea (common morning glory)
Vessel: Antique | Roman glass
Season: Summer

Common morning glories are a typical summer flower known by everyone. By arranging the flower on the opposite side to the freely extending leaves and vine, I was able to draw out slightly negative elements such as shame and sadness. Depending from which angle the flower and iridescent vessel are viewed, their color appears gradated, creating an impression of rebellion that is itself beautiful.

Lilium Concolor

The star lily is also commonly known as the fairy lily. In its native habitat it's often called the princess lily. A pretty plant, it does not grow very tall, reaching about two feet (half a meter or so).

In order to accentuate its ephemeral air, I arranged it so that the stem extended straight up from the small mouth of the vessel. I allowed the leaves to trail down to match the downward-facing flower. The gentle natural curve of the stem and the fragile balance of the weight of the downward-facing flower combined with the small vase create an arrangement evoking scene of flowers blooming quietly in the hills and dales.

Flower: Lilium Concolor (star lily)
Vessel: Antique | Vietnam | Small green glazed jar
Season: Early Summer

Campanula Punctata

The spotted bellflower is a wildflower that blooms in early summer in much of the East. It is also cultivated in many parts of both East and West. It is said to get its Japanese name of "firefly bag" from the long-ago children's game of putting fireflies into the blooms. The variety used for this game is the garden type grown in flower beds. I was attracted by the deep purplish blue of the flowers. The straight, upright figure of the flower standing in the vase of the same color evokes the dignity of summer wildflowers. As the mouth of the vase is wide compared with the slender stalk of the bellflower, it is kept in place with a single twig across the opening.

Flower: Campanula Punctata (spotted bellflower)
Vessel: Ikigata Yuka | Ceramic | Vase
Season: Early Summer

Lilium Leichtlinii
var. maximowiczii

Lilium leichtlinii var. maximowiczii grows in mountain meadows of cooler regions. It is a lily defined by its boldly-curled back petals and its mottled markings. It grows straight from the roots up, but curves abruptly near the neck of the flower. This change in direction and the withered leaves at the base give it the look of an original species, so rather than hiding them I incorporated them into the arrangement.

Flower: Lilium Leichtlinii var. Maximowiczii
Vessel: Artist unknown | Korea | White porcelain vase
Season: Summer

Sorbus Commixta

The autumnal red fruit and colored leaves give this
Japanese rowan allure. It has large branches, so is a
floral material often used for fall decorations.
The Japanese name of "nanakamado" (seven hearth
firings) comes from the wood being so strong that it
can withstand seven firings in the hearth without
burning. In actual fact the wood burns well, so there
is probably another derivation for the name. In order
to make the fruit-laden branch the star of this
arrangement, I let the branch spring out in front of
the vessel. I chose a black vessel to keep it low-key.

Flower: Sorbus Commixta (Japanese rowan)
Vessel: Antique | Karatsu ware | Sake bottle
Season: Fall - Winter

Coreopsis Lanceolata

Flower: Coreopsis Lanceolata (lanceleaf tickseed)
Vessel: Antique | France | Truffle bottle
Season: Spring - Summer

As an invasive species that robs native flowers of their habitat, the lanceleaf tickseed has become a target for extermination. I found this one in the riverbed near my home. It caught my eye because the stem section had petrified.

Because I arranged the plant to highlight the impressively winding flat, petrified stem, the flower faces backward when the arrangement is viewed from the front.

Chapter 2

LIGHT AND FLOWERS / CREATING A NATURAL ARRANGEMENT

The Direction of Light

Plants have a tendency to move toward light. They grow by facing the sun, extending their flowers and stems in the direction of light in order to perform the photosynthesis necessary to their survival. Even plants that grow in shade grow as if moving in the direction of the sunlight. Hanaike that take into account the direction from which light enters make people feel comfortable. This is because they follow the natural order of things, so there is no sense that something is out of place. The term "natural style" is often used to describe "a way of arranging that is not elaborate in taste," but hanaike that matches the plant's natural ecology is the real definition of natural style.

When creating hanaike, clearly visualize where the light is coming from and where the sun is so as to consider the direction of the flowers you are arranging.

Light and Position in the Tokonoma

(Alcove for displaying art or flowers)

The unique expression of Japanese flowers was cultivated in spaces such as the *tokonoma*, which is enclosed on three sides. Among tokonoma, the "hon katte" style has lighting from the left side, while the "gyaku hon katte" style has lighting from the right. It's usual to have light entering from one side in this way, either the left or right.

When flowers are viewed in the tokonoma, they are viewed from front-on. As the room is generally a tatami room, the flowers are viewed from a seated-on-floor position; one does not stand to look down on the flowers. The way the light enters therefore needs to be considered with this in mind. Where the flowers are being viewed from is also a very important point in hanaike. Even when not displaying them in a tokonoma, it's important to arrange them by considering the "vantage point" of the viewer and look at them from that line of vision.

Turning Away From the Light

There is no need to match all hanaike to the direction of the light. If you have a form you want to express or show, even if it defies the laws of light, you can do it in the reverse. Taking human emotions as an example, when one is feeling down, one wants to avoid bright light, and hanaike is the same. Facing an object toward the light is a straightforward, easily understood way of expressing natural form.

By facing a flower away from the light, depending on the look of the flower, it's possible to create the expression of a solitary, powerful figure, making it ideal for those times when you want to express an inward, melancholy atmosphere or a rebellious spirit.

Light as Staging

In the natural world, the way light enters is basically from above—from the sun. In human consciousness, light comes from the sky. In contemporary architecture, the light comes not from the sun but from lighting that can be controlled by humans. As is clear through its use in theatrical performances and so on, lighting can be used to create effects. For example, light from above has the effect of accentuating objects in the same way as the sun. Light shining from below distorts objects and emphasizes their presence.

This use of light from above and below can have the complete opposite effect from that which is understood by human consciousness. In the case of the musical play *Jekyll and Hyde* in which one person plays two roles, by lighting the gentle Jekyll from above and the villain Hyde from below, light can be used to communicate not only the actor's ability to act, but also the differences between the two personalities. Essentially, light can be used as staging to convey expression in a way not impossible in everyday life. Using the surface of water or a mirror placed below an object to reflect light from above can also create a unique expression.

Camellia Sasanqua

Flower: Camellia sasanqua
Vessel: Nishikawa Satoshi | Ceramic | Vase
Season: Winter - Spring

This camellia flowers earlier than camellia japonica. I like the sasanqua as much as the japonica.

I found a rare single-layered flower. Compared with the flamboyant multi-layered type, the single-layered flower makes a modest impression, but its single core gives the sense of strength. I arranged it to boldly face in the direction of the light. The branch is held in place like a spring in the cracked edge of the vase.

Wild Tulip

Flower: Tulipa tarda
Vessel: Antique | Copper | Fire pan
Season: Spring

Tulips continue to follow light even after blooming. I used two flowers from a dwarf species that is considered a wild variety, arranging them to nestle close together. In the dim space, both seeking the light, the beauty in their fragile appearance revealed itself. The vessel is an old fire pan, the lid of which keeps the base of the flowers in place.

Clematis
"Duchess of Edinburgh"

I'm very partial to clematis. For this arrangement, I used a clematis that I grew myself.

The flower is boldly turning toward the light, but the leaf is shaped so that its reverse side is facing upward. In reality, this would not happen due to the direction of the light, but the shape of the leaf drawing closer to the flower was interesting and I wanted to emphasize this look.

Flower: Clematis "Duchess of Edinburgh"
Vessel: Antique | China | Stoneware
Season: Spring - Summer

Fritillaria

Fritillaria verticillata var. thunbergia and *Fritillaria camtschatcensis* are classified in the genus *Fritillaria*. The flower in this arrangement is also in this genus, but its cluster of small, hanging bell-like flowers give it a slightly different air.

I found the form of the stem bending upward to pursue the light interesting and chose a vessel that would play up this aspect. Using a vessel in the same color as the flowers accentuates the movement of the stem and focuses attention on the flowers.

Flower: Fritillaria
Vessel: Antique | Uganda | Milk pot
Season: Spring

Crataegus Cuneata

Beginning its show of color in the fall, the Japanese hawthorn is a plant in the genus *Grossulariaceae*. It is not related to the edible hawthorn, which is a member of the rose family.

The branches with clusters of small fruits reach out horizontally toward the light before extending upward. The fruits tend to change color from where they are exposed to light, so keep this in mind when creating an arrangement.

Flower: Crataegus cuneata (Japanese hawthorn)
Vessel: Goryeo │ Black glaze │ Salt chest
Season: Fall

Anemone

Even as cut flowers, anemones are extremely susceptible to changes in light, opening and closing their petals depending on light and temperature. Here, I've found an anemone whose posture evokes that greedy search for light.

As the petals are white and the core and vessel are both black, the result is a unified monotone arrangement that creates a beautiful figurative expression.

Flower: Anemone
Vessel: Kumagai Koji | Earthenware | Vase
Season: Winter - Spring

Pueraria Montana var. lobata

I used a vigorously growing kudzu vine for this arrangement. These days, kudzu are treated as weeds, but originally their roots were used medicinally and as food. The subdued purple flowers have an air of elegance.

The flowers that rise up from the trailing vine as if to express the kudzu's strength piqued my interest. While the flowers are turned firmly toward the light, one of the leaves curves toward the left, expressing this plant's lack of straightforwardness and its wild resilience.

Flower: Pueraria montana var. lobata (kudzu vine)
Vessel: Antique | Uganda | Milk pot
Season: Summer

Aconitum, Pueraria Montana var. lobata

Here, I've used kudzu that, having finished flowering, has just started to fruit. I combined it with the beautiful but poisonous wolf's bane.

The kudzu is a vine that grows by winding itself around other plants. A close representation of a natural scene is achieved here, with the kudzu growing entwined with the flowering wolf's bane. Apart from those that are necessary, the leaves of the vigorous kudzu have been removed and the arrangement has been shaped to show the flowers' beauty. The vessel used is earthenware from China. As its mouth is wide, I've used a thick twig to hold the arrangement in place.

Flower: Aconitum (wolf's bane), Pueraria montana var. lobata (kudzu vine)
Vessel: Aoki Ryo | Ceramic | Black glazed jar
Season: Summer

Ipomoea Purpurea 2

In comparison with the morning glory of ancient times in Japan, the common morning glory flowers until the afternoon, so it could be said that it is suited to hanaike. The stem extending out from the decanter creates a smooth curve, with the flower at its tip turning decidedly toward the light. I chose a glass vessel in order to show the vine entwined around the base of the stem.

Flower: Ipomoea purpurea (common morning glory)
Vessel: Azuchi Tadahisa | Glass | Decanter
Season: Summer

Cosmos, Chestnut

Here, I've chosen two materials that are typical of the time of year when fall begins to make itself felt—a cosmos flower and chestnuts. Both are in season in fall.

I've placed two lush green chestnuts in the mouth of the antique inkstone water vessel and arranged a pretty cosmos flower between them. The cosmos has its reverse to the light and faces downward. Its gentle refusal of light creates a fragile expression.

Flower: Cosmos, chestnut
Vessel: Antique | Old Seto ware with seal engraving
Season: Fall

Ribes Rubrum, Paederia Scandens

Flower: Ribes rubrum (redcurrant), Paederia scandens
Vessel: Antique | America | Earthenware

The creeping *Paederia scandens* winds around the branches of the redcurrant. They are facing away from the light, but this results in the movement of the tip of the *Paederia scandens* creating the most attractive position. The goal of hanaike is not to always face flowers toward the light, but rather to orient flowers in an arrangement that lets them really shine.

Making corrections to the branch of the redcurrant before winding the *Paederia scandens* around it achieves a beautiful line.

Tulip

Here, I've deliberately used a tulip—a flower that has a strong tendency to face the light—as an expression against light. The stem of the tulip has been curved to follow the curve of the vessel. As the vessel does not have a stable base, I've used a small stone as a platform against which to lean it on an angle. The vibrant color of the tulip flower is accentuated by the dim world inside the vessel.

Flower: Tulip
Vessel: Antique | Iron | Pot
Season: Summer

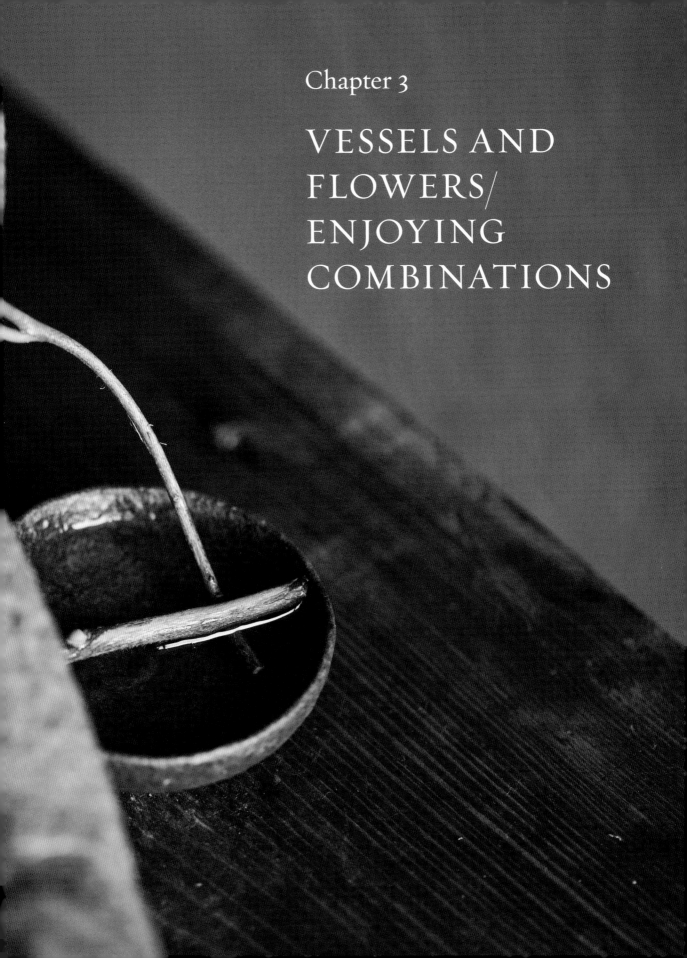

Chapter 3

VESSELS AND FLOWERS/ ENJOYING COMBINATIONS

How to Choose a Vessel

As with choosing flowers, the most important factor when choosing a vessel is whether it stirs your emotions. Even if they are both made from glass, you can choose a transparent vessel or one with a cloudy, frosted look. There's a wonderful variety of shapes as well as of materials. The choice of vessel can change depending on one's taste and one's mood at the time. I believe one should use one's senses to choose.

In hanaike, there is an extremely close relationship between the vessel and the flowers. Rather than what type of vessel to select, it's important to decide whether to start by choosing the flowers or the vessel. If selecting flowers first, a vessel that brings out their attractiveness to the utmost is crucial. Consider whether to make the color of the flowers the focus or to lean toward their size or shape when pairing them with a vessel. If selecting the vessel first, consider the approach from the vessel to the flowers. Give some thought as to how you want to show the flowers and what is possible in relation to a particular vessel, and choose the flowers that best convey your thoughts.

There are no right answers when it comes to hanaike. Look at the choice of flowers and vessels carefully and consult with yourself to make your selection.

Knowing Your Vessels

The connection between vessels and flowers is deep and inseparable. I myself often work together with ceramic and glass artists, arranging flowers at their exhibitions and holding showings with them. It gladdens me to see that, with the recent popularity of ceramics, there are more and more people who are familiar with vessels made by artists. Surely there are also more than a few people who began flower arranging with vessels as their starting point. Artists' work and traditional craft pieces have different roots, and it's good to play that up when creating hanaike. However, not knowing about a vessel is not a problem. Just as with flowers, once one becomes interested in them, they can be researched. What is important is the thought behind choosing the vessel, why particular flowers were chosen and one's intended expression in an arrangement. If those emotions are present, your hanaike will impress even those who are knowledgeable about vessels.

Color Matching

I also consider the color combination of vessels and flowers. Broadly speaking, the color matching configurations that people find attractive can be divided into two types. The first is gradation, where colors of different intensity in the same shade are matched. The second is contrast, where complementary or opposite colors are combined. Depending on how these two types are configured, an attractive expression will result.

For instance, in order to express softness, flowers from white to pink may be placed together, with just a hint of green from a fruiting branch added to the arrangement. This creates a charming air. The first layer is a gradation of pale colors, with the green fruits overlapping as contrast in the second layer. This manner of overlapping several materials is called "layering." It's important to create variation, so if the first, or base, layer is of starkly contrasting colors, the second should feature gradation.

These two types of color configuration are layered to fit the color of the vessel and flowers. When one is still learning, there's a tendency to go overboard with both the floral materials and vessels and use too many materials. Overlapping too many materials obscures the object one initially wanted to show, so take care to avoid using too many layers.

Matching Form and Color

I use gradation and contrast as the two methods of color matching, but you can also use these two broad types to divide form. In terms of form, gradation can correspond to softly curved lines. Gradation means the gradual change of color tone and brightness, so it refers to the gradual arcing of a stem.

Regular flowers have a fine, straight stem with a large blossom blooming at the end. This serves as "contrast." For example, if a stem and flower are around the same thickness, contrast is lacking and few people would find the flower attractive. People experience surprise and an awareness of beauty from the sudden presence of a large flower form on a slender stem. Clematis and other flowers I especially like also have extremely slender stems with large flowers, a perfect balance of flower and stem. It stirs the emotions to think that such a fine stem could put forth such a beautiful flower.

Trientalis Europaea, Viola Mandshurica

In this arrangement, the northern starflower, a wildflower with an air of mystery, plays the leading role. I positioned two violet leaves of similar texture in the mouth of the vase and placed the flower between them. Matching the color of the flower and vessel accentuates both the sophisticated air of the vase and the neat prettiness of the flower.

Flower: Trientalis europaea (northern starflower),
Viola mandshurica (violet)
Vessel: Morioka Kiyoko | White porcelain | Vase
Season: Spring

Narcissus Pseuodonarcissus, Wild Tulip

This little old glass inkwell is a found piece. The center section that holds a pen is not particularly roomy, so I thought it would be best to use something that would create a miniature worldview to match the size of the vessel.

I chose a wild daffodil flowering in a pot and wrapped the base in the leaf of a wild tulip to achieve a unique, adorable arrangement.

Flower: Narcissus pseuodonarcissus (wild daffodil), wild tulip
Vessel: Antique | Glass | Inkwell
Season: Spring

Campanula, Carrot

Although the main flower is a campanula, it is one of the smaller cultivars. As there is a unique balance between the long, slender stem and the flower at its tip, I created an arrangement that would properly show the stem. The vessel I chose is an old French wineglass. As the vessel is glass a twig or other similar device wouldn't be suitable to hold the stem in place. Instead, I cut the flowers of a carrot and placed them in the water for this purpose.

Flower: Campanula "Pixiebell", carrot
Vessel: Antique | France | Wineglass
Season: Summer

Smoke Tree, Flannel Flower

Here, I've paired a slim earthenware vessel with a voluminous piece of smoke tree. Viewed from afar, there is a symmetry between these flowers and the vessel, the reason being that their similar colors blend them together. The flannel flower placed in the center and the pale green of the smoke tree's leaves bring out a brightness that creates highlights in the arrangement.

Flower: Smoke tree, flannel flower
Vessel: Antique | Syria | Earthenware
Season: Early summer

Narcissus Jonquilla 2

When creating an arrangement in a clear glass, work according to the fact that the inside is visible. It's possible to make slight tweaks to bulb plants such as the narcissus jonquilla. Here, the white section from the bulb to the stem, which already has a curve to it, has been slightly balled up to place inside the vessel, with the turned-back bulb serving to stabilize the stem. It's an arrangement that displays how the flower is held in place, which is not usually shown.

Flower: Narcissus jonquilla
Vessel: Antique | Glass | Small jar
Season: Winter - Spring

Camellia Japonica, Spathodea

The buds arranged together with the camellia are from the
spathodea, also known as the African tulip tree. I was attracted by
their unique form. To provide contrast with the calm tones of the
vessel and spathodea, I chose a white camellia, arranging it to
emerge from the back of the spathodea to face straight out in front.

Flower: Camellia japonica, Spathodea
Vessel: Antique | The Netherlands | Glass bottle
Season: Winter

Eriocapitella Hupehensis, Lithified Edamame

The unique green plant is a lithified edamame. With its winding stems, thick, flat stalks, and occasional brown hairs, it is full of rugged vitality. The Yayoi-style earthenware vessel paired with this powerful edamame has a simple strength. Adding the typical flower form of the single Japanese anemone that is in such stark contrast to these two elements serves to balance the overall feel of the arrangement.

Flower: Eriocapitella hupehensis (Japanese anemone), edamame (soybean)
Vessel: Yayoi era earthenware reproduction
Season: Fall

Camellia Japonica 2

With the right kind of handling, any kind of
vessel can be used for hanaike. Here, I've paired
a gorgeous multi-layered camellia blossom with
a shrine guardian-like dog ornament, arranging
them to create the sense that the flower and dog
are looking at one another. When arranging
flowers in this kind of ornament, the set-up is
important. Here, another vessel is placed
behind the ornament to contain water and the
flower. Take care to select a vessel whose size
and shape allow it to stay hidden when the
arrangement is viewed from the front.

Flower: Camellia japonica
Vessel: Antique | Ornament
Season: Winter - Spring

Flower: Zinnia Barbie Mix
Vessel: Nishikawa Satoshi | Ceramic | Medium
and small pots
Season: Spring - Fall

Zinnia Elegans

With their large blooms and fine petals, colorful zinnias have a presence that makes one's heart flutter just from looking at them. Here, I've chosen colors that create gradation from red through to pink. The vessels selected are two different sized pots in a duller red than that of the flowers. I placed the flowers in the small pot with the other one on top to hold them in place. In order to bring out the unique form of the petals, the flowers are arranged to face slightly to the side rather than straight ahead.

Hardenbergia

With small flowers that form "ears," the Hardenbergia (also called lilac vine) is similar in shape to the Phalaenopsis aphrodite and is a member of the legume family. I selected a black antique vessel to set off the purple of the flowers, adding water into the vessel and using the displaced section of lid to hold the Hardenbergia in place. I let the flowers trail down to follow the outline of the lid.

Flower: Hardenbergia
Vessel: Antique | China | Unglazed pottery | Lidded receptacle
Season: Spring

Linaria, Sedum

Combining the pale blue of the vessel, the faint green of the
sedum and the gentle quality of the small flowers, I created
this work to have a gentle worldview. While the Linaria is
tilted toward the sedum, it is also firmly oriented toward the
light. The beautifully executed ridges of the vessel have the
effect of slightly offsetting the sweet air of the flowers.

Flower: Linaria, Sedum burrito
Vessel: Kamiizumi Hideto | Porcelain | Ridged cup
Season: Spring

Pansy

This vessel in attractive silver foil is an objet created to recall a lotus leaf. For this arrangement, I started with the vessel and chose a pansy, whose petals are frilled and resemble the form of the vessel. The vessel has a beautiful color and form, so in order to draw those out I chose a calmer, quiet flower.

Flower: Pansy
Vessel: Hayashi Michiyo | Silver foil | Objet
Season: Spring

Flannel Flower

Here I've matched a flannel flower whose petal tips are a fresh green with a small pot made in Thailand. The flower arranged at the mouth of the vase has unique coloring. The flower opens out from the vessel, creating the appearance of the next flower growing out from it.

Flower: Flannel flower
Vessel: Antique | Sangkhalok | Ceramic ware | Small pot
Season: Summer

Chapter 4

BEING AWARE OF GRAVITY / MAKING USE OF BRANCHES AND STEMS

Gravity

Everything that lives and exists in this world must have energy. If, like humans, other beings have the power to resist gravity, they can stand up to the workings of that force. But if they are not alive, they lose the energy to defy gravity, gravity takes over, and they are left lying there.

Plants and humans alike rise from the surface of the ground. Most plants stand up in the search for light. They then move barely at all from the place where they were born, and where their life ends. They are extremely modest and reserved. They don't utter a sound. The Japanese people, who have been living a settled lifestyle since rice cultivation began, must have deeply empathized with plants' perseverance. Back in the day, for most Japanese people, continuing to live in the same place was a sign of life. I believe the reason ikebana culture became so established in Japan was because of the sympathy and empathy Japanese people feel for plants in their own lives.

In order to create beautiful hanaike, it is important not only to combine the shapes and colors of the vessels and flowers, but also to connect and express the flow of inherent energy of each flower in a beautiful way.

Hanaike and Gravity

In the world of ikebana, "capture the essence" is a commonly used phrase. It means to arrange flowers with an understanding of their center of gravity. It is not only in ikebana that what humans perceive to be aesthetically balanced is often based on what is real, and this reality is the center of gravity. Many built forms have gravity-defying energy flowing upward from the center of gravity.

I said before that living beings have the energy to resist gravity, but the same is true of matter. When we place matter on the ground or in contact with other surfaces, energy is generated. By creating an arrangement in a vessel, the plant is able to acquire the energy from the vessel. By properly capturing the essence of the vessel and plant, it is possible to create a flow of energy.

Visualizing Energy

In dynamic hanaike, curved flowers, twigs and stems are often used. The curve in twigs or stems results from the changing movement of the plant during its growth process. A plant that normally would grow straight up and flow to the left may instead grow vertically before extending down and then growing out to the side. This is the trajectory of the plant's search for light. In hanaike, skillfully playing up such traits brings movement to an arrangement. It's also possible to create a work in which the plant appears to be moving by acquiring energy from the vessel.

When you capture the essence of a vessel to arrange flowers, the direction in which the ends of the twigs or leaves or even the tips of the flowers end up pointing is the direction in which the acquired energy will flow. Be conscious of your ability to visualize the energy when you want to create a dynamic expression or indicate a plant's natural growth.

Shaving Off

In hanaike, the twigs and leaves of floral materials are often removed. Twigs in particular are a floral material that can convey the flow of energy in a more dynamic manner. Just as for selecting flowers in chapter 1, it's important to note that twigs have individual differences. Start by choosing those that are closest in form to what you most want to express. Even within a single branch or twig, there can be both powerful and weak sections. Effectively bringing out the strongest, most unique section of the branch makes it possible to attract people's attention. In order to do this, remove the unnecessary, unattractive twigs and leaves one by one. It's fine to do it all at once, but when you're uncertain it's best to check the form so as to avoid mistakes. If you make an effort to bring out a simple, neat line in the twig or stem, not only will the flow of energy become clear but the resulting form will be attractive.

Camellia japonica 3

In contrast with the pretty flower, the base of the
thick branch shows a trajectory that calls to mind
the twists and turns involved in the plant's growth.
I have arranged the plant to appear as if it is
gradually reaching from the rustic-looking pot in
the search for light. Removing some of the leaves
reveals the strong will of the flower.

Flower: Camellia japonica
Vessel: Kutsuzawa Sachiko | Ceramic | Objet
Season: Winter - Spring

Celastrus Orbiculatus, Angelonia

This hanaike emphasizes the curve of the Japanese bittersweet's slender branch. It moves in a leisurely way toward the light as it extends up from the vessel, then finally turns away from the light. Its unrestrained, light flow of energy is clearly communicated. Placed in the section at the base where the fruits cluster, the angelonia serves as an accent.

Flower: Celastrus orbiculatus (Japanese bittersweet), Angelonia
Vessel: Antique | China | Small pot
Season: Fall

Paeonia Obovate

I found a woodland peony that was just about to shed its blossom. Standing erect before experiencing a major refraction, its earnest effort to grow upward creates a unique form. In order to express this flow I chose a funnel-shaped vessel. As if resisting the energy to reach upward, the downward-trailing petals and leaves convey the plant's ending.

Flower: Paeonia obovate (woodland peony)
Vessel: Antique | Japan | Objet
Season: Spring

Solanum Jasminoides

There were mottled yellow leaves growing on this
Solanum jasminoides branch, but in order to
emphasize the movement of the stem, I removed
them as I created the arrangement. If it's not
necessary to do so, I prefer not to remove twigs,
leaves and so on. In this case, having the leaves
would lead to a vague-looking arrangement, so
while monitoring the effect, I removed them. The
delicate movement of the slender stem is
accentuated by the translucent, understated flowers.

Flower: Solanum jasminoides
Vessel: Unknown artist | White porcelain | Sake cup
Season: Fall

Aquilegia, Akebia Quinata

Complementing the movement of the branch, the dynamic energy comes across in this hanaike. The branch of the chocolate vine stands erect before the power to grow vertically completely changes course to suddenly cascade down. Adding a single, neat columbine flower to the place from which the energy is rising creates a worldview in which power is moving to protect the flower.

Flower: Aquilegia (columbine), Akebia quinata (chocolate vine)
Vessel: Antique | India | Candlestick

Pine, Camellia Japonica

I cut off a long upper section of pine and used a sharply
angled branch in the main role of the arrangement. The root
section of the pine sits above the mouth of the vessel. This
creates the appearance of the roots' energy being stored in
the vessel, then rising powerfully up to flow toward the light.
Inserting the camellia into the space created by the
movement of the branch has a softening effect on the space.

Flower: Pine, Camellia japonica
Vessel: Antique | Mino province | Iron-glazed sake bottle
Season: Winter

Tristellateia Australasiae

Rather than using whole branches of Australian gold vine, I have trimmed the whole stock to use. As the ends of the branches are all neatly turning in the direction of the light, I arranged them to bring out this appeal. An interesting flow of force was created, as if the power from the center of gravity exploded and radiated out all of a sudden to each branch.

Flower: Tristellateia australasiae Million Kiss (Australian gold vine)
Vessel: Antique | Joseon dynasty | White porcelain | Small pot
Season: Fall

Flower: Cucumber "shakitto"
Vessel: Aoki Ryo | Yakishime | Sake bottle
Season: Summer

Cucumber

This is a piece of cucumber plant cut from the main stock. The stem of cucumber plants is soft and rich in moisture, giving it a different look from twigs or flower stalks. Here, I have played up the sinuous undulations that typify plants in the cucumber family. By incorporating the large leaves into the arrangement rather than removing them, I have allowed the dynamic interest of the plant to remain.

Violet

In this simple, attractive vessel, I've arranged a single fragile violet.
The heart of this hanaike is the vessel opening. The violet catches
the energy released from the vessel as it rises and falls. It's
important not to miss the minute expression in this vessel.

Flower: Parma violet
Vessel: Kuroda Taizo | White porcelain | Vase
Season: Spring

Cosmos, Pueraria Montana var. lobata

Here, I've matched a native kudzu vine with a cosmos, arranging the flower to nestle at the base of the branch. The branch rises up from the vessel's center, gathering strength as they spiral upward.

Flower: Cosmos, Pueraria montana var. lobata (kudzu vine)
Vessel: Tsuruno Keiji | White porcelain | Teacup
Season: Fall

Hardenbergia 2

Here, I've chosen a large, round vessel. In contrast with its size, the vessel is made to have a small mouth. I've integrated the arrangement with the round shape in order for it to receive energy from the vessel in an unaltered state.

Flower: Hardenbergia
Vessel: Anzai Kenta | Vase
Season: Spring

Nelumba Nucifera

Two lotus flowers are arranged on top of each other in the vessel, creating a unique form. I have created the look of the lower flower emerging from the pot and taking on its energy, striving to rise upward, so have been conscious of the force extending directly above. Additionally, the sense of distance between the flowers and the mouth of the vessel was important in this work.

Flower: Nelumba nucifera (lotus)
Vessel: Kuroda Taizo | White porcelain | Vase
Season: Summer

Linaria, Iris Ochroleuca

The Linaria and Iris ochroleuca are arranged to rise straight up from the center of the pot. It was difficult to stand the plants in the pot as they were, so I placed stones in the base to secure them. Rising straight up, the Iris ochroleuca expresses the graceful strength of the pot.

Flower: Linaria, Iris ochroleuca
Vessel: Antique | Iron | Pot
Season: Spring

Chapter 5

BALANCE / THE BALANCE OF BEAUTY

The Balance of Beauty

I think an attractive balance in hanaike changes depending on the expression. Perceptions of beauty also differ from viewer to viewer. As I mentioned with regard to matching colors, the layering of several elements or materials is the basic foundation of beauty, but too much layering creates an excess and blurs what you are trying to convey.

It's important not to forget your initial intuitive sense of beauty and the materials (flower, pot and color) that you selected with that beauty in mind. You need to have a grasp of each material. Even if you intend a particular expression and have envisioned it accordingly, if the materials chosen are unsuitable, the arrangement will lack balance.

My way of hanaike is as simple as as it gets. This is because even if only one flower is used, it is possible to convey beauty. Using many flowers or incorporating a variety of techniques into an arrangement creates something that is gorgeous, but may be far removed from simple beauty and emotion. Be sure to come back to basics. Treasure and appreciate the sense of a flower's beauty in order to ask yourself what it is that you want to convey in hanaike.

Being Interesting

I regularly conduct hanaike lessons overseas and within Japan. During those lessons, a phrase I often use is "That's interesting." Perception of what is interesting varies from person to person. For me, a thing is often interesting if I perceive it to have a unique form. Humans have a tendency to empathize with those in similar circumstances or whose way of thinking sympathizes with their own. I think I'm a little different. It's difficult to be an oddball. The surrounding winds are strong and hard to bear. I wish I could live comfortably, but I have to endure and live in a cruel environment. This projects onto the flowers as well. Even if flowers lined up at the flower market appear the same at a glance, looking carefully, some are facing out to the side and some are downcast. When I encounter flowers such as these, I wonder what their lives were like before they ended up here, waiting to be purchased.

The form and size of plants are influenced by their environment. Whether they've been grown in a place with strong winds or have once been stepped on, it's these plants that have grown up adapting to a harsh environment that I find appealing, and I make an effort to face these flowers in order to make the most of their characteristics.

Decision Work

When I was young, I was "harder" than I am now, and projecting myself onto flowers was not possible. I was not able to "layer" myself onto such a pretty existence as that of a flower. This made itself evident in my expression work; I was only able to project myself onto things such as rusted iron, aged metal and stone. As the years went by and I experienced setbacks, married and had a family, this changed and I became more empathetic toward flowers.

In hanaike, beauty is the axis or point on which we base various decisions. As mentioned previously, what kind of flowers, light, vessels, colors and so on one chooses and how one combines them are decisions that must be made in each situation. Get rid of preconceived notions toward vessels and flowers and face them using only beauty and authenticity as decision points. Apart from that, it's important to just take things as they come.

Places to Display Flowers

The best place to display flowers is somewhere that they can be viewed from the same direction as that in which you arranged them. Japanese floral culture has developed uniquely in the *tokonoma*, a space enclosed on three sides. Requiring a strong sense of frontality, this space has led to a demand for the creation of strongly frontal forms. It could also be that human nature seeks frontality in all things, which in turn gave rise to the form of the tokonoma. Either way, hanaike are not very suited to places such as dining tables from which they can be viewed from all four sides.

However, these days not many people live in a dwelling that has a tokonoma. A similar kind of place is a space with a wall behind it. For example, placing hanaike on a chest or desk alongside a wall makes it easier to convey the thoughts of the person who arranged it. They should also not be viewed from a far distance. As there are few flowers in a hanaike, I recommend placing them somewhere where they can be viewed face to face.

Anemone 2

As long as they stir your heartstrings, I think it's fine to use flowers in hanaike even if they are not in an attractive condition. This anemone has lost several petals, but by pairing it with a porcelain vessel in the same color, it is possible to create a somber expression.

Flower: Anemone
Vessel: Kuroda Taizo | White porcelain | Vase
Season: Spring

Camellia Japonica 4

Half multi-layered camellias in full bloom are arranged to be viewed from directly in front, with the plump flowers placed as if tilted toward the edge of the vessel. Aligning the mouth of the vessel and the direction of the flowers and making the leaf tips angle upward makes for a forward-facing expression.

Flower: Camellia japonica
Vessel: Unknown artist | Ceramic | Lipped vessel
Season: Winter - Spring

Hydrangea, Clematis

This hanaike expresses the sense of fullness and volume in the in-season hydrangeas. There is no need for a device to secure the flowers, as they are held in place by the hydrangea stems. The clematis emerging from the hydrangeas appears to be blooming by drawing energy from the vessel.

Flower: Hydrangea, Clematis
Vessel: Antique | Seto ware | Brazier
Season: Early summer

Celosia Argentea

Plumed cock's comb is one of the flowers I find I can project myself onto. Here, I've arranged two stems of lithified cock's comb one on top of the other. The velvet texture of the cock's comb is the complete opposite to the glossiness of the vessel, but the tones are all gradations of the same colors. An interesting expression of confict arises from the combination of contrasting textures and related tones..

Flower: Celosia argentea (plumed cock's comb)
Vessel: Tsuruno Keiji | Yakishime | Vase
Season: Summer - Fall

Hydrocotyle Vulgaris, Campanula

This hanaike makes use of the unique form of the vessel, with the vessel and flowers creating a natural shape as if integrated. The delicacy of the campanula and the unique shape of the marsh pennywort make for a pleasing expression.

Flower: Hydrocotyle vulgaris (marsh pennywort), Campanula
Vessel: Antique | White porcelain | Lighter
Season: Summer

Nelumba Nucifera 2

Once cut, lotus leaves dry out right away, tending
to curl inward. Here, I've arranged leaves that have
not yet completely dried out together with a flower.
The differences in color and texture of the leaves'
surfaces and undersides and their interesting shape
stand out.

Flower: Nelumba nucifera (lotus)
Vessel: Aoki Ryo | Ceramic | Powdered metal urn
Season: Summer

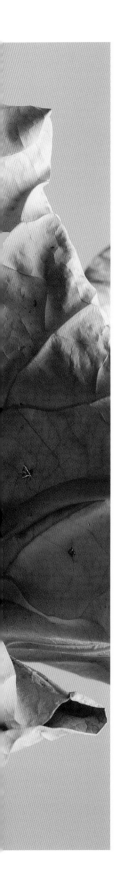

Fritillaria, Aspidistra

Here, I've wrapped a Fritillaria in a withered brown Aspidistra leaf. The good thing about using dried items is that the range of expression broadens as there's no need to consider water absorption. The rising dead leaves resemble the wings of a flapping bird, giving the work a unique air.

Flower: Fritillaria, Aspidistra
Vessel: Antique | Thailand | Small ash-glazed jar
Season: Spring

Rose

Here, I've arranged roses that are just about to dry
out. They are not in an attractive condition, but I
thought I would like to express the decay suggested by
their appearance. I put the browning petals together
with a vessel that is chipped around the opening.

Flower: Rosa (rose)
Vessel: Unknown artist | Unglazed pottery | Waste-water container
for the tea ceremony
Season: Fall

Chapter 6

TECHNIQUES FOR PERSONALIZING HANAIKE

Hitomoji—one stroke

This is the technique most often used in this book. It involves wedging a single twig across the mouth of the vessel to hold flowers in place.

Using the twig means that even if you arrange flowers in a vessel with a wide mouth, they will remain standing straight. It is also useful for keeping flowers in the same position within an arrangement.

A work in which the hitomoji technique has been used. Standing the *Hypericum chinense* to stand straight up out of the mouth of the vessel makes the bold arch shape of the branch clearer and accentuates its presence. If the hitomoji had not been used, the plant would lean against the mouth of the vessel and the form of the branch would be unattractive.

Using a vessel with a wide mouth, such as a teacup, for displaying flowers makes it difficult for them to stand up straight. Adding a twig to the center holds the stem in place and directs the flower as a whole upward.

Inserting a twig to form a hitomoji

1 Fill the vessel with water until it is about 70% full, then use your hand to wedge a piece of cut twig horizontally across the mouth of the vessel, slightly below the opening. You don't have to confine this method to twigs; a stiff piece of stem is fine too. Cut it to a length so that it wedges exactly into the opening. It's quite difficult to alter the length, and even if it is only slightly too short, the twig will fall into the bottom of the vessel, so practice this effective technique over and over to master it.

Place the stalk of the flower into the space created by dividing the vessel with the twig. The stalk should be placed in the space farthest from the direction in which the flower is facing. Placing it there creates space between the vessel and the plant.

2 Once you have arranged the flowers, pour more water into the vessel. The reason for keeping water low initially is to avoid spills when the twig is being wedged in.

3 Once water is poured into the vessel, the presence of the twig is not immediately obvious, as this photo shows. The twig only plays a supporting role, so if you use a twig or stem in a similar color to that of the vessel, the vessel will help conceal it. For example, if the vessel is white, using a bleached Edgworthia chrysantha (paper bush) twig will create a subtle finish.

Hanaike using hitomoji

Ever since it bloomed in the flower bed, this flower has been gradually collapsing, but adding a hitomoji to prop it up at the base accentuates the gentle curved line of the stem.

Despite creating a unique curve, this flower is oriented decidedly in the direction of the light. In order to express the dynamic movement of the stem and flower, it is necessary to boldly lift the base of the stem. The twig used for the hitomoji has been peeled so that the bark does not detract from the color of the vessel.

Jumoji—Cross or Crucifix Form

As its name suggests, *jumoji* is a way of securing flowers that involves adding a twig to a hitomoji to create a cross shape over the opening of a vessel. It's a technique that is employed when using many flowers or when flowers are to be viewed from all four directions. It is not used in the works in this book. Like hitomoji, jumoji has the effect of raising the flowers from the vessel. There is more work involved around the mouth of the vessel compared with the hitomoji technique, so it's a good method to use for vessels with large openings.

Inserting twigs to form a jumoji

1 Use two twigs to form a cross at the mouth of the vessel. This allows the opening to be divided into four spaces. The methods for choosing the twigs and pouring the water into the vessel are the same as for the hitomoji technique.

2 Insert the first flower, working the stem into the opposite direction from that which the flower will face.

3 Add in the second flower. The key point here is to insert the stem in the space opposite from that of the first flower. The flower's orientation is in contrast to the space in which the stem is placed. By using this technique, not only is it possible to secure the orientation of several flowers, but as with the hitomoji technique, it allows space to be created within the vessel and among the flowers and branches, expanding the range of possibilities for your work.

OPPOSITE: This work brings out the sense of volume in a blossoming mimosa. Using four stems of mimosa and inserting one stem into each of the four divisions created by the jumoji creates a work that is attractive from all directions. If the jumoji technique were not employed, the vessel and flowers would be too close, preventing a sense of dimension and making for a heavy impression. Using the right method for securing flowers draws out the mimosa's charm and appeal.

Securing flowers with wire

This *hanadome* (means of securing flowers) involves balling up wire and placing it inside the vessel. The balled-up wire creates partitions that support the flower stems. This technique is suited to vessels that have wide mouths and some depth to them. It is useful for times when you want the flowers to stand up straight or express a sharp angle, and is suitable for flowers that do not have thick stems, or for fine twigs and branches.

Balling up the wire

1 Ball up a long piece of wire so that it fits inside the vessel and is concealed by it. If it is too small in comparison with the vessel, the wire will move around, so adjust the size. Here, copper wire has been used, but metals such as aluminum are fine too.

2 Once you have placed the wire inside the vessel, insert the flowers into the wire. Here, they are inserted straight into the center section, but it's also possible to place them in on an angle.

OPPOSITE: A gloriosa that is flowering at the end of a stem that has branched off from the main stalk. In order to express the fact that the flower has been grown in a field, it is inserted straight into the securing device. As the stem is delicate, it would be difficult to secure the flower in the wide-mouthed vessel without a hanadome, but the ball of wire creates firm support.

Techniques to bring out height

Even when components are compatible for what you want to express, there are times when the length of the flower doesn't balance properly with the vessel. You've probably also had the experience of trimming off too much of a stem or branch. These are techniques that are useful in such situations.

Inserting into a twig

If the material you are using is not long enough, split a twig and insert the plant into the gap. This is a technique from olden times known as "soegi tome" or "splint clasp." It serves not only to add height, but can also be used in combination with the hitomoji technique to stabilize materials within a vessel.

Here, I'm creating an arrangement with a platanus, but its original length was insufficient so I have sandwiched the end into a twig to create height.

I've trimmed a cucumber flower at its base to arrange it, but as it is not long enough to create the form that I want, I've used a bamboo skewer to create height.

Inserting a bamboo skewer

Inserting a soft flower stem into a split twig will squash the stem, so use a bamboo skewer instead. Cut the skewer a bit longer than the length to which you want to extend the stem and poke it into the stem. Adjusting the length of the skewer allows you to adjust the height.

Hanadome using stones

It's possible to substitute stones in the role of hitomoji twigs. This is effective in vessels with narrow openings or where it would be difficult to insert a hitomoji twig.

Place stones at the mouth of the vessel in accordance with where you want the flower to be oriented, then arrange the flower to lean on the stones. Unlike the hitomoji device, it's not possible to conceal the stones inside the vessel, so consider the stones as part of the hanaike for display and take care when selecting their color, size, texture and so on.

Techniques that make use of the vessel

The form of the vessel and the way it is used broaden the range of expression. The way of using the vessel alters depending on the desired expression. Here we look at some examples.

Leaning the plant against the vessel

In order to express the daintiness of the glossy red berries, I arranged them without using a hitomoji, simply allowing them to hang over the vessel, nestled against the edge. It's an extremely simple technique.

Using cracks in the vessel

This vessel is cracked in one section, but as it is not leaking, I poured water into the vessel and let the flower emerge from the cracked section. Similarly to plants that bud from gaps in asphalt, this creates an expression of resilience.

Using the lid

This technique is recommended when using a lidded vessel rather than a vase. Slightly shifting the lid from the vessel and arranging the flower in the gap created secures the flower in place.

Stacking two vessels 1

Here, two vessels of the same shape are stacked one on top of the other, with the flower secured between them. The unstable appearance of the stacked vessels is, in this case, part of the work. It's also important to add water to the vessel on top.

Stacking two vessels 2

Here, two differently sized vessels by the same artist are stacked one on top of the other. The leaves are secured in the overlapping section in the same way as in 1, but here, flowers are arranged in the upper vessel as well.

List of vessel artists

Aoki Ryo

Azuchi Tadahisa

Anzai Kenta

Ikigata Yuka

Kamiizumi Hideto

Kutsuzawa Sachiko

Kumagai Koji

Kuroda Taizo

Tsuruno Keiji

Nishikawa Satoshi

Noto Asana

Hayashi Michiyo

Morioka Kiyoko

About Jikonka TOKYO

The vessels used for hanaike in this book were loaned from the range available from Jikonka TOKYO in Setagaya-ku (ward), and some of the photography was carried out in their Japanese-style room.

With shops in Kameyama City, Mie prefecture, and Setagaya-ku, Tokyo, Jikonka is written in Japanese characters as 而今禾. 而今 (jikon), which means "at this moment," while 禾 (ka) is a general term for grains, an indispensable food for life, something of great importance. The name basically means "how we live at this moment." Jikonka is a gallery selling original clothing and food items along with ceramics and various crafts and antique vessels. It aims to be a place where people can learn about life and living through clothing, food, and housing. Jikonka TOKYO also regularly hosts Ueno Yuji's hanaike classes.

Jikonka TOKYO
7-15-6 Fukasawa, Setagaya-ku, Tokyo
Tel and Fax: 03-6809-7475
Email: tokyo@jikonka.com

Closed: Tues, Wed, Thu and for long holidays
Opening hours: 13:00-18:00
www.jikonka.com

Index

Note: For those plants whose botanical/alternate name differs from the one used in this book, the Latin is also provided.

Afterword

Just like humming a tune, hanaike should be easy and fun. No one needs basic singing technique in order to hum. Humming is the desire to sing springing forth, kind of like breaking into a dance without even thinking about it.

I made this book for people who love flowers and would like to try arranging them. I hope it will help many people bring flowers into their daily lives and arrange them creatively.

Arranging flowers is a form of play. It's important to enjoy it with a light heart. Placing a single flower in the mug you usually drink from might change the way you look at life.

I'm sincerely grateful for the opportunity to share with you through photos and text my knowledge of flower arranging. I hope you found the experience to be a lovely one.

My deepest thanks to Sakurai Junko, the writer who so carefully edited my clumsy words in the crafting of this book. This book resulted from the collective effort of many talented people, including photographer Nomura Masaharu, who made excellent use of natural light to create the beautiful photographs; Nishikawa Hironobu of Jikonka, who assisted with the vessels as well as with the photo shoots; book designer Takanashi Hitoshi and everyone at Seibundo Shinkosha Publishing. To all of them, my utmost gratitude. Thank you so much.

—Yuji Ueno